"Insightful, clear an[illegible] an excellent introduction to Mark's [illegible]pel. Ruth explains things that might be unclear to somebody reading and studying the Gospel for the first time – her long experience of introducing people to Jesus in a multi-cultural city is evident. The Lord Jesus' identity is clearly seen, as is our need to respond to him. I warmly recommend this book and I hope it will be widely used."

Wallace Benn, Former Bishop of Lewes and Founding Chairman of Bible by the Beach

"This little book will help you read and understand Mark's Gospel with a month of tasty bite-sized chunks."

Michael Ots, Speaker and Author

"This helpful little book has such an accessible approach to reading through Mark's Gospel in one month, enabling the reader to encounter the living Jesus. The key ideas provide you with an ongoing meditation to take into your day and the beautifully crafted prayers allow the Gospel to become rooted in your life."

John MacKinnon, Director of Evangelism, The Word One to One

"If you're looking for a clear, simple guide to reading the Bible for the first time, this is it. Ruth Bridcut welcomes the reader into the Gospel of Mark, laying out the main points and giving just enough context to smooth the way. The short prayers of response helpfully mark this journey of understanding who Jesus is and what he came to do."

Kathleen Nielson, Speaker and Author

"The Bible contains sixty-six books written in different genres over nearly 2,000 years – unsurprising we can struggle to open our Bibles and know where to start. *Unlocking Mark's Gospel* is a treasure if that is you. As you journey through Mark's Gospel in thirty-one days, Ruth will not only help you understand the essence of each section you are reading, but draw you closer to the glorious and wonderful God who loves you."

Alistair Chalmers, Pastor of Ferniehill Evangelical Church

Unlocking Mark's Gospel

Ruth Bridcut

10 Publishing
a division of 10 of those.com

First published in Great Britain in 2023

British Library Cataloguing in Publication Data
A record for this book is available from the British Library

ISBN: 978-1-914966-63-7

Designed by Hannah Beatrice

Printed in Denmark

10Publishing, a division of 10ofthose.com
Unit C, Tomlinson Road, Leyland, PR25 2DY, England
Email: info@10ofthose.com
Website: www.10ofthose.com

Introduction

Many people find it daunting to read the Bible for themselves, simply because it is unfamiliar. This book is therefore intended as an aid for anyone feeling unfamiliar with the Bible.

Mark's Gospel is a good place to start reading the Bible because it is the shortest of the four Gospels, which recount Jesus' life and teaching. Mark concisely and clearly presents us with the Jesus of history – what he said and did.

This book is not intended as a stand-alone book. Rather, it will be of greatest help if you begin each session by reading the relevant section of Mark's gospel and then use the notes to help you think more about what Mark has written.

While this book is intended to help you read the Bible and discover more about Jesus, the comments are not vital for your understanding. If you wish to read the Bible text alone, I'd encourage you to do so. You could read Mark's Gospel straight through in about an hour and a half. Alternatively, you could use the sub-divisions I've chosen to read a little at a time over the course of a month.

However you read Mark's Gospel, I pray that you will discover that the Bible is not inaccessible at all! Rather, I pray that you will enjoy discovering new things about Jesus – who he is, why he came and what it means to follow him.

Who was Mark?

Mark wrote his Gospel approximately thirty years after Jesus died. He was a friend of Peter, who was a close friend of Jesus and a source of much of the eye-witness material which Mark recounts. Mark's Gospel is one of three other accounts of Jesus life, death and resurrection in the Bible, with the others written by Matthew, Luke and John.

The gospel accounts may include some terms that are new to you, but these are explained in a glossary at the back of the book.

How can I find my way around Mark's Gospel?

Mark's Gospel was originally written as one document. However, for ease of reference, it was later divided into sixteen chapters (often printed as a large number in our texts) and each of those chapters was divided into verses. Sections of the Gospel are referenced by the chapter and verse numbers. For example, Mark 2:3–6 refers to a section of text from Mark chapter 2, beginning at verse 3 and ending with verse 6. Individual verse numbers within a particular chapter are indicated by the abbreviations 'v.' or 'vv.' (for example, v. 1 or vv. 14–16).

While chapter and verse numbers were added afterwards by Bible editors, they can be a useful way of referencing and remembering key sentences within the text. At the beginning of each session of this book, there is one verse from the relevant section of the gospel. You may find it helpful to try remembering this during the day as you reflect on what you are reading.

A note on prayer

We can pray to God about many things – our needs, the needs of others, things for which we are thankful and other things for which we are sorry. We can also pray using either our own words or pre-written prayers. The prayers in this book are designed to help you pray about what you have read in the corresponding passage from Mark's Gospel.

God reveals himself as three persons in one, for example at Jesus' baptism (Mark 1:9–11). We can call God our Father and pray directly to him because Jesus has made this relationship possible. However, it is often appropriate to pray directly to Jesus or to the Holy Spirit. All such prayers are to the same 'three-in-one' God. Thus Jesus instructed his followers to pray:

- to God the Father. (The most well-known example of this is the Lord's Prayer, which begins, 'Our Father in heaven'.)[1]
- in the name of Jesus. (That is why we often end such prayers by saying, 'in Jesus' name'.)
- through the power of the Holy Spirit.

---

1 See Matthew 6:9 and also Luke 11:2.

He's here!

The beginning of the good news about Jesus the Messiah, the Son of God …

Spoiler alert! Mark answers the question 'Who is Jesus?' in his opening sentence!

Jesus is the Messiah and the Son of God (v. 1). The name Messiah means a rescuing King for God's people, and was promised long ago in the Old Testament by prophets such as Isaiah.

In this passage we also meet John the Baptist, who calls people to turn away from their sin and goes about in the wilderness baptising people. All humans face the problem of their sin – ignoring God and his commands. Baptism is a ceremony of washing with water to symbolise the washing away of sin that is possible for all who confess their sin. John is the messenger about whom Isaiah prophesied and who is to prepare the way for the Lord Jesus (v. 3).

The Lord is described by John as one more powerful than he – John isn't worthy to untie his sandals (v. 7)! Finally, the Lord is coming!

How should people get ready for his arrival? Not by laying out a red carpet. Instead, John calls for an inner heart preparation – repentance. That is, all people are urged to be sorry for and turn away from their old sinful way of life, and instead to turn towards God's way.

Jesus is baptised by John, but as a voice from heaven declares him to be the Son of God (v. 11), we know he had no sin to turn from. Jesus really is the promised Lord with a message of good news: 'The kingdom of God has come near. Repent and believe the good news!' (v. 15).

What is the good news? God's rule is going to be seen more clearly. The arrival of his long-promised King marks the beginning of God's rescue of us from sin, death and evil.

How should we respond to this good news of a rescuing King? We should be open to recognising who Jesus is, to turning from our sin and to believing this great news.

God has entered into the world he made and calls people to believe in him.

KEY IDEA

Mark's Gospel is all about good news. Jesus the Messiah – God's promised, rescuing King – is worth believing and following.

PRAYER

Dear God, thank you that Jesus – the promised, rescuing King – has come into our world. Please help me to understand more of this good news as I read Mark's Gospel, and especially to know more about who King Jesus is. Amen.

Who's the boss?

> *The people were amazed at his teaching, because he taught them as one who had authority, not as the teachers of the law.*

There's a new celebrity in town, creating endless good-news stories of healings and freedom from demon possession. There's no fake news in the reports about him, and his popularity is growing!

Jesus has previously said that the kingdom of God is drawing near (v. 15), meaning God's rule will be more visible. He doesn't mean rule over a geographical area, but rule in people's lives. What will life under Jesus, God's King, look like? Jesus gives a glimpse of this as demons are overpowered, sickness is overcome and he teaches with an authority different from the religious teachers of the time. Today we still face evil and sickness, but one day this glimpse of Jesus' rule will be a universal reality.

Most of Jesus' audience are impressed by him but don't understand who he is – except the evil spirits. They are threatened as they recognise the power and authority of the one they call 'the Holy One of God' (v. 24). However, Jesus silences them when they shout this out.

Why does Jesus not want the demons broadcasting his identity? He is focused on his mission of spreading his kingdom by preaching the good news. A high-profile celebrity status would hinder this (as happens later, for example in verse 45).

The crowds begin to flock to Jesus, but he withdraws to pray. He won't be dictated to by crowds or demons; he must focus on the mission he has come to fulfil.

Why does Jesus not stay where he is popular and heals constantly? It's because he's the boss! His priority is to spread the good news. Jesus does amazing things to help many people, but his own agenda has priority.

This poses a challenge for us. Do we recognise Jesus has authority in this world and over our lives? Or do we just have a passing interest in his words and actions? Let's resolve to take his authority seriously as we listen more to what he said and did.

KEY IDEA

Jesus sets the agenda as he teaches, heals and drives out demons. With all his authority, he still sets the agenda today!

PRAYER

Dear God, thank you for Jesus bringing in your rule in a new way, with the authority of God himself. Thank you for this glimpse of a future time with no more sickness or evil. Please help me to take Jesus' authority in this world seriously as I read more of what he said and did. Amen.

Sick or healthy?

... the Son of Man has authority on earth to forgive sins.

If we know we're sick, we go to the doctor for help, hopeful for a cure. The man with leprosy, a contagious skin disease, knows he is sick and knows someone who can cure him.

But he wasn't just physically sick; he was classified as spiritually unclean and excluded from the community. He knows Jesus can heal him, but will he? Jesus is more than willing. He makes the man clean, both physically and spiritually in the eyes of God.

What sickness plagues the man on the mat? All can see he is paralysed, but Jesus first cures his spiritual sickness – he pronounces that the man's sins are forgiven (2:5). The teachers of the Jewish law are horrified. 'Who can forgive sins but God alone?' they think to themselves (2:7).

Any sin is ultimately against God, so Jesus has just claimed to do something which only God can do – blasphemy! Has Jesus the authority to forgive sins, the authority of God himself? After all, anyone could say those words, but how can we know it is a reality?

Jesus tells the man, 'Get up, take your mat and go home' ... and he does! (2:11–12). Jesus proves his authority to forgive by healing the man. So Jesus has authority to forgive us too! Have you asked him to forgive your sins?

The Pharisees (one kind of Jewish religious teacher) are good at spotting sin and spiritual sickness in others (2:16), but think they are healthy themselves (2:17). We need to recognise our problem of sin and ask Jesus to forgive us – he can and will!

KEY IDEA

Jesus is more than able and willing to forgive us and make us spiritually clean, if we are willing to come to him for help.

PRAYER

Dear Jesus, thank you that you were concerned about the paralysed man's greatest problem of sin and had power to help. Thank you that you have power to forgive my sins too. Help me to confess my sin to you and then to rest in the peace of your forgiveness. Amen.

A new era

... the Son of Man is Lord even of the Sabbath.

Everything about Jesus is different from the norm. Why? He's bringing in a totally new era. As such, he's like a bridegroom, so now is not a time for fasting. Like a new patch on old cloth or new wine in old wineskins, Jesus' new way doesn't fit into the old – everything is being renewed. But this makes upholders of the old status quo (like the Pharisees) very uncomfortable.

In particular, Jesus challenges their approach to the Sabbath, a sacred day of rest. The Pharisees believe that picking grain to eat is harvesting and therefore a work task that is forbidden on the Sabbath. In contrast, Jesus heals a man with a shrivelled hand on the Sabbath because his priority is to 'do good' (3:4).

Who gives Jesus the right to renew the use of the Sabbath? He simply declares that right himself in declaring himself the Son of Man, an Old Testament title for someone like God. As Son of Man, Jesus is Lord, or ruler, even of the Sabbath (2:28)!

Not surprisingly, this causes a reaction and brings together two unlikely groups of people. The Pharisees and Herodians (supporters of King Herod) are united in a plan to do away with Jesus...

Are we aware of the radically new way of thinking and living which Jesus brings? How much are we willing to follow Jesus' ways rather than the voices and traditions of our day? Is there a danger that we may be stubborn in response to Jesus' teaching (as the people are in 3:5)?

Let's ask God for hearts that are willing to listen to and follow Jesus even when his teaching may be new to us.

KEY IDEA

As Lord, Jesus teaches us a new way of thinking and living. How will we respond?

PRAYER

Dear God in heaven, thank you for Jesus' example of not letting other people stop him from doing good to others, no matter what day it is. Please help me to be willing to listen and follow Jesus' teaching even if it's new and different from my old ways. Please continue to teach me more about Jesus as I read the Bible each day. In Jesus' name, amen.

Whose side is he on?

Whenever the impure spirits saw him, they fell down before him and cried out, 'You are the Son of God.'

News of this healer, teacher and exorcist is going viral, and he is gaining a cult following. The impure spirits know who he is ('the Son of God', v. 11), but Jesus orders them not to tell others.

Why would he resist fame? As discussed before (see session 2), Jesus knew that if the Jewish people heard who he was, they would expect him to bring political deliverance and this focus would hinder his mission.

Meanwhile, Jesus gathers a group of twelve, sending them out to preach and to drive out demons (vv. 14–15). Why twelve? These disciples are a new version of the twelve tribes of Israel, the Old Testament people of God.

Jesus is popular in some quarters, but others aren't convinced. 'He is possessed by Beelzebul!'(v. 22) and 'He has an impure spirit' (v. 30), they say. Where does his power come from? Jesus forces them to stop and think!

If Jesus really were using power from Beelzebul, the prince of demons, why would he be destroying demons? The idea that Jesus would perform miracles by Satan's power isn't just ridiculous; it's blasphemous. Jesus declares that anyone who says he has an evil spirit is blaspheming God's Holy Spirit, the third person of God the Trinity.

We each need to decide what we think about Jesus and his power. Is he holy, with the power of God, or is he from the devil?

Maybe you have slandered Jesus in the past – this can be forgiven (v. 28). But we must heed the warning about a continuous, deliberate blaspheming of him or his Spirit (v. 29).

Even if we don't slander Jesus, we can't remain indifferent. If he really is the Son of God, then he has power over Satan and his weaker kingdom.

Jesus' biological family don't understand him (v. 21), but we need to decide which side we are on.

KEY IDEA

Jesus shows his power over Satan and his weaker kingdom, so he is stronger than any evil power today.

PRAYER

Dear Jesus, thank you for helping me to see how scandalous it must be for you that we might fail to recognise you as coming from God. Please help me not to slander you. Instead, may I rejoice that you are stronger than evil and the devil, and may I understand more about your true identity. For your glory I pray, amen.

Listen!

Whoever has ears to hear, let them hear.

'Whoever has ears to hear, let them hear' (v. 9). That applies to everyone, surely? Well, not necessarily. Jesus begins telling his parable (a story with a hidden meaning) with the challenge: 'Listen!' (v. 3).

Jesus' parable seems fairly straightforward – a farmer scatters seed which falls on different types of ground, resulting in varying harvests. Are you interested to think more about the parable? Not everyone is, but the Twelve and some others do ask Jesus about his parables. He explains more, namely the 'secret of the kingdom of God' (v. 11) to those willing to listen.

When Jesus says that his parables will be understood by those who have ears to hear, he is quoting the Old Testament prophet Isaiah (see Isaiah 6:10). There will be no understanding for those on the outside, who don't take time to enquire more. Yet there is lots to learn for those who want to know. Jesus' parables have a filtering effect.

So let's listen up to the explanation! The farmer is sowing the word of God. The different soils are different kinds of people who hear this word and respond differently. Some have it snatched away from their minds; some take heed for a short time, but are distracted by troubles or worries; others hear the word, accept it and produce a crop, meaning they grow in faith.

Which kind of soil are you like? Are you prepared to stop, to listen, to think about Jesus' words and to allow his words to change you? That's how to be like good soil!

KEY IDEA

We can have ears which are deaf to Jesus' words or we can choose to listen, allowing his words to sink in and to change us.

PRAYER

Dear God in heaven, thank you that you reveal secrets about your kingdom through the Bible to those who want to listen. Please help me to have a heart which wants to listen to Jesus' words and to accept them. Please would other ideas and distractions not pull me away from listening to you. I pray that many others also would not have hard, inattentive hearts. In Jesus' name I pray, amen.

The power of words

Who is this? Even the wind and the waves obey him!

How do you learn best? Some of us learn visually; others through doing; still others through listening. Jesus continues teaching in a range of ways – through the parables he tells and the actions he performs.

In this passage, Jesus teaches his followers four mini parables related to the kingdom of God. Do you understand them (see verse 33)? Firstly, in God's kingdom there is no place for deceptive or secretive actions (vv. 21–23); all will one day be brought into the open before God. Secondly, there's a responsibility on the listener to use the measure of knowledge and understanding that they have been given to gain more, or they may lose it (vv. 24–25). The last two parables describe how God's kingdom grows. Should we expect a viral response to Jesus and his teaching? Like a growing crop or a mustard seed, the growth is largely an unseen, slow effect, but it will grow to be very large.

Jesus then teaches through practical experience. Notice it was Jesus' idea to cross over to the other side of the lake with his disciples (v. 35). A storm breaks out, the waves crash over the boat and it's nearly swamped, but Jesus sleeps! The helpless disciples wake him in a panic, but do they really know what they expect him to do about the problem? When Jesus calms the storm with a few words, they are not relieved that they survived; instead, they are terrified (v. 41)! They have had a glimpse of who Jesus is – someone whom even the wind and the waves obey.

How do you feel about Jesus, the Son of God, being able to control the forces of nature with a few words? People living with Jesus as their King may not seem significant or impressive, but the King they follow is a force to be reckoned with! Pause to consider the power you see Jesus exert in this passage.

KEY IDEA

Jesus has the power to calm a raging storm with a few words – that is literally awesome!

PRAYER

Dear Jesus, I'm amazed at this glimpse of your power over nature. Help me to remember your power in those times when I may feel overwhelmed. Please help me to grow in my understanding of who you are as I listen to you speak in the Bible. Amen.

Power over evil

Go home to your own people and tell them how much the Lord has done for you, and how he has had mercy on you.

Now in a non-Jewish region, Jesus meets a man in torment. The man is physically free, having resisted all attempts to tie him down, yet he seems to be imprisoned. How can this be? His tormented actions are explained by his conversation with Jesus – he is controlled by impure spirits who speak on his behalf and identify themselves as Legion, a term used for many Roman soldiers.

The many spirits have authority over the man, but why do they throw the man to his knees before Jesus, begging for mercy? They recognise Jesus has a greater authority and that they need Jesus' permission regarding where they may go. Jesus permits them to enter a large herd of pigs. Wonderfully, the man is restored – he is clothed and in his right mind (v. 15).

Yet there is no community celebration for this man. Instead, the people ask Jesus to leave. Jesus has displayed such awesome power and authority that the people are afraid. In contrast, the man, who has received an amazing blessing of freedom and mercy, has amazing news to share![2]

Jesus is more powerful than the strongest forces of evil, visible or invisible. Does this fill you with fear (like the people) or faith (like the restored man)? We might not often see explicit evidence of evil today in the same way. However, we can be encouraged that no matter what happens in

---

2 Jesus has previously tried to suppress news of his miracles becoming widespread, as otherwise the Jews would flock to him as Messiah, detracting from his purpose of preaching (see 1:38). However, in the Gentile (non-Jewish) region of the Decapolis, Jesus encourages the spreading of news about his activities.

our personal lives or on the world stage, Jesus has authority over Satan and unseen evil forces.

KEY IDEA

In our world there is not an equal battle between good and evil – Jesus always wins!

PRAYER

Dear Jesus, thank you that you showed yourself to be the Lord, with authority over evil. Thank you that you cared about this man and restored him to his right mind. Please help me to trust your greater power as I see the effects of evil in the world. Help me to be like that man, trusting your awesome power and eager to tell others. Amen.

SESSION 9 Mark 5:21–43

Power over sickness and death

The child is not dead but asleep.

Twelve years is a long time, especially if you've been suffering from a chronic menstrual bleeding problem, and have become poor through spending so much on doctors. For this woman, it has also made her socially and ritually unclean. (Under Jewish law, an emission of menstrual fluid or semen made a woman or man unclean for social and religious purposes.) Twelve years is also a long time to love and care for a precious daughter, only to see her desperately ill and close to death. This is the case for Jairus, a leader in the synagogue (the Jewish place of worship). Both the sick woman and Jairus are in desperate situations. Who do they turn to for help? Jesus. In doing so, their faith in Jesus is not unfounded, but deepened.

They learn first that Jesus cares. Both the woman and Jairus are aware that Jesus has the power to heal, and are trusting that he will do the same for them. Wonderfully, the woman is healed of her bleeding, but why does Jesus insist on interacting with her? It is because he also cares about her spiritual well-being. He doesn't want her to think that he is an impersonal, automated, supernatural force. Rather, he rewards her personal faith in him.

Just as Jesus cared for the woman, he cares for us in our sufferings and struggles.

But does Jesus care for Jairus too? In the delay since Jairus pleaded with Jesus to heal his daughter (vv. 23–24), she has died. There is an outpouring of grief and emotion. However, Jesus cares about Jairus' spiritual well-being too. Jairus is therefore to learn that Jesus can raise the dead. Jesus' statement that 'The child is not dead but asleep' (v. 39) is naturally received with ridicule. But how easy is it for Jesus to raise the girl from the dead? Just like we might rouse someone from sleep!

Jesus has power over death today. For the person who believes in him, death is not the end. The Bible describes the death of a believer as sleep; believers will sleep until Jesus returns to make all things new.

What comfort these truths bring!

KEY IDEA

Jesus cares about our suffering and death, and he has power to overcome them.

PRAYER

Dear Jesus, thank you that you have compassion on those who are sick and struggling. Thank you that you have power to heal sickness, and power over our final enemy, death. Please help me to trust you and to grow in faith if I or others I know go through such difficult times. Amen.

A radical mission

They went out and preached that people should repent.

'Is he related to so-and-so?' We like to know who people are, connecting them with others we know, putting them in a box in our minds. The people in Jesus' home town know his family, but Jesus' teaching, wisdom and miracles just don't fit. Radical teaching coming from one of their own isn't well received. Jesus is not the first to be rejected by those closest to home (v. 4).

Jesus' family and friends thought they knew him, but his teaching isn't what they expected. Do you have any presumptions or prejudices about Jesus which are being challenged as we read Mark's Gospel?

Undeterred, Jesus multiplies his ministry by sending the twelve disciples out to other towns and villages. They are not to take anything with them, but their needs will be supplied by those welcoming them.

However, not all will be favourable to them or their message. When the disciples meet such hostility, they are to respond by shaking the dust off their feet to show those in the town that the disciples are no longer responsible for them. They are to 'wash their hands' of those who reject the message, who ignore the call to repent – a call to turn from sinful ways and instead live to please God (vv. 11–12).

Followers of Jesus today are also called to repent. In what ways would your life change if you turned from sinful ways of living towards God's way? It's not easy (which is why many ignored Jesus and his followers), but it's worth it if we remember Jesus' identity. He is the Messiah, the Son of God, not just some local bloke!

KEY IDEA

Jesus' message isn't always comfortable – he calls for repentance, a turning from sin to follow God's ways.

PRAYER

Lord God, please help me to have a right attitude to Jesus and his teaching. Help me not to be prejudiced, but to recognise he is the Son of God. Help me also to repent – to be sorry for sinful ways of living and to live with Jesus as my Lord. Help me to grow in understanding of who Jesus is so that I see why following him is worth it. Amen.

Life in the kingdom can be costly…

… Herodias nursed a grudge against John and wanted to kill him.

Jesus and his disciples are calling people to repent – to turn from their sinful living. When King Herod hears this, it triggers his memory – it isn't long since John the Baptist gave him the same message. Things hadn't ended well then – Herod had ordered John to be beheaded.

Perhaps his guilt explains why Herod wonders if Jesus is John the Baptist returned from the dead (v. 16). In explaining the backstory, Mark shows us the implications of the call to repent, to turn from sin.

Herod and Herodias – his brother's wife, whom he then married – resist the call to repentance. John had been confronting Herod about how his love life was not in line with God's laws. The woman in question, Herodias, nursed a grudge and wanted to silence John. Herod himself recognised John as living a morally right life (righteous) and being holy, and so liked to listen to him. Yet the call to repentance didn't impact him either. Instead, Herod's failure to obey God caused him to walk into a trap of his own making. To spare his reputation, Herod was forced to kill John. Because of Herod's pride, John's call to repentance cost him his life.

Jesus has just told his disciples that there will be times when people will not welcome them or listen to them (v. 11). However, this incident shows us that turning to follow God's ways may be even more costly. John cared more about honouring God and living his way than the opinion of those with human authority and influence.

How about us? Whose opinion do we most value? Are we willing to turn to follow God's ways? John's story illustrates how, by doing so, we will find ourselves going against the surrounding culture, which may have costly consequences.

Is the call to repent therefore worth following? Yes, because it involves turning to trust the God of the universe. He is the loving God who sent his Son, Jesus, to rescue us from our problem of sin and who has ultimate power and authority – not only now, but for eternity!

KEY IDEA

Repenting and following God's ways may be costly, but eternally is worthwhile!

PRAYER

Lord God, please help me not to ignore truths about you, or your call to repent, as Herod did. Rather, please help me to understand more about what it means to follow your ways. Please help me to know and understand more about Jesus and his message, so that I may have godly priorities and be willing to put you first, whatever the cost. Amen.

Comfort in crisis

Take courage! It is I. Don't be afraid.

After their missionary endeavours, Jesus encourages his disciples to rest. That's easier said than done! Jesus is moved by the sight of the large crowd who are 'like sheep without a shepherd' (v. 34). How does he respond? He teaches! Later that day, it's the disciples who will learn the most...

Jesus teaches he has the power of God to provide. Initially, Jesus challenges the disciples to feed over five thousand people in a remote place – but how can they, with little food or money? When Jesus again urges them to see what food they can find, the disciples follow his instructions and gather five loaves and two fish. The disciples see Jesus give thanks for the food and break the loaves. They then distribute food to all the people. Astonishingly, 'They all ate and were satisfied' (v. 42). Afterwards, the disciples pick up twelve basketfuls of broken pieces – one each.

The disciples may have remembered how God provided bread (manna) for their ancestors in the desert in Old Testament times (see Exodus 16). Did they learn the lesson here? According to verse 52, they did not understand.

Jesus immediately sends them out in the boat, to teach them he has the power of God over nature. They are straining against the wind when they see a ghost, walking on the water. They are terrified and then amazed as they recognise Jesus' voice and the storm is stilled! Jesus has the power of God!

Jesus' words to them – 'It is I' – are the same 'I am' phrase which God used in the Old Testament. God declared, 'I am who I am' (Exodus 3:14) when revealing himself to Moses, a leader of God's people.

Jesus is teaching that he has the power of God himself. The disciples don't understand fully, but even through their confusion and in the midst of crisis, Jesus comes alongside saying, 'Take courage! It is I. Don't be afraid' (v. 50).

Isn't this a comfort for us in times of crisis? Jesus has the power of God himself, and if he is with us, we need not be afraid.

KEY IDEA

With the authority of God, Jesus says in a crisis, 'Take courage! It is I. Don't be afraid.'

PRAYER

Lord Jesus, thank you for showing us and the disciples your power and presence in times of crisis. Please help me to grasp more of how you have the power of God. Please also help me to have a heart that responds to you, so that I can trust you more. In times of crisis, may I be comforted by your power and presence with me. Amen.

How clean are you?

What comes out of a person is what defiles them …

I hope you wash your hands before you eat! In this passage, Jesus isn't being accused of being unhygienic. Rather, his disciples are criticised for being lax on the traditions of ceremonial cleanness. The Jewish leaders are concerned with moral contamination by touching unclean items such as non-Jewish food or people. Such traditions are high on their list of priorities.

But couldn't it be that following outward traditions, however good, can become more important than inwardly seeking to follow God? Have you ever seen (or been…) a hypocrite, honouring God outwardly, but inwardly having a heart far from him (see verse 6)? Jesus gives the example of the Jewish tradition of 'Corban' (v. 11). By this, money is declared as ring-fenced for God. However, the problem is that this money is then not spent, as it should have been, on supporting a person's parents. This heart attitude is far from the God who commanded his people to honour their parents (see Exodus 20:12)!

Jesus goes on to teach that spiritual uncleanness doesn't come from outside, but from inside a person. He lists all-too-familiar emotions which bubble up from our hearts (see verses 21–22). How do you fare, as you compare what comes from your own heart with the evil things in Jesus' list?

Once any of us are guilty of any of these evil things, Jesus says we are 'defiled' or 'unclean'. This is a sobering truth for us all. Our sin, which bubbles up from within our hearts, is a serious problem, but that's why news of a rescuing Saviour is so good!

KEY IDEA

Our spiritual uncleanness comes from our hearts, which is the problem Jesus came to fix!

PRAYER

Heavenly Father, it is sobering to think that we are unclean because of the evil attitudes and deeds which bubble up within us. As you know, I particularly struggle with [list those that apply from verses 21–22]. I am guilty of being a hypocrite. I seem nice on the outside, but you know my sinful heart. I'm sorry for all the ways I have not pleased you. Please help me to grasp how serious this is. But please help me also, as I continue to read Mark, to grasp how Jesus can make me clean. I pray in his name, amen.

SESSION 14 Mark 7:24–37

Outsiders are welcome too!

> *... as soon as she heard about him, a woman whose little daughter was possessed by an impure spirit came and fell at his feet. The woman was a Greek ...*

Sadly, every society has people and groups which don't fit in and feel excluded. Not so with Jesus – he makes a point of going into areas to meet people who aren't normally made to feel welcome.

The Greek woman is desperate for Jesus to help her possessed daughter. She seeks Jesus out and isn't put off by his reminder of how society views her – she is not a Jew (a child of Israel) and is more than aware that other Jews view those like her as dogs. Indeed, she expects Jesus to think the same, and yet she hopes that even dogs might get a share of his blessing.

What does Jesus actually think of the woman? Let's remember that he has deliberately come to this area and has just been teaching that what's on the outside of a person isn't what makes them unclean. Jesus' response to the woman about tossing bread to dogs (v. 27) is not demeaning, but acknowledging society's attitude. The woman's reply then displays her inner faith and humility – her inner heart attitude, which is what matters. Jesus commends this – and the demon leaves her daughter.

The Decapolis was another region inhabited mainly by non-Jews. Jesus spends time there with individuals, such as the deaf-mute man. His ears are opened and he can speak freely. Jesus has time and compassion for all people, irrespective of their social standing.

This presents us with encouragement and a challenge. If you feel an outsider compared to others in your local Christian community, remember that Jesus has time and compassion for all people, irrespective of their background. But perhaps you need to be challenged to think whether there is anyone you feel Jesus might not welcome or who is not respectable enough? Jesus seeks out and knows individuals. He calls them, irrespective of their place in society, to put their faith in him. Let's be willing to welcome all whom Jesus welcomes.

KEY IDEA

No matter what society or even the church may think, Jesus welcomes all who come to him in faith.

PRAYER

Lord Jesus, thank you that no matter how we may feel different because of our ethnicity, background, ability or any other reason, you welcome anyone who comes to you. Please help me to respond to you with a faith like the woman's. Like the man, please open my ears to hear you clearly. Amen.

Do you see?

Who do you say I am?

'Do you see?' said my maths teacher so many times, yet he wasn't concerned about eyesight! The numbers and symbols were plain to see, but it was a different story to 'get it'! Jesus has a similar question for the disciples: 'Who do you say I am?' (v. 29). That is a question for each of us too!

There is no lack of miraculously provided bread or fish to see when Jesus feeds four thousand. Yet the Pharisees don't see who Jesus is and ask for 'a sign from heaven' (v. 11). Are the disciples much better? They have now seen two miracles of multiplying bread, yet they still don't understand their significance! Have the Pharisees and King Herod infiltrated their thinking, like yeast in bread (v. 15)? Or could they have hard hearts (v. 17)?

With so many barriers to seeing, it's no surprise that the only man who sees clearly does so because of a miracle. Jesus lays his hands on the blind man and restores his sight. The blind man sees gradually – first people just look like walking trees, but then he sees everything clearly when Jesus once more puts his hands on the man's eyes. We know Jesus can heal immediately, so could he have been illustrating here the spiritual miracle necessary for anyone to 'see'?

What does Peter see about Jesus? Through a spiritual miracle, Peter can see Jesus is the Messiah (or Christ) – God's promised, rescuing King.

How do you see Jesus? Special intelligence won't help us see who Jesus is, because we are naturally spiritually blind. But we can see Jesus really is God's rescuing King when God miraculously opens our eyes! Let's ask God for help so that we and others we know see clearly who Jesus is.

KEY IDEA

If we have eyes yet fail to see, it will take a work of God for us to see Jesus clearly.

PRAYER

Dear Jesus, thank you that you can make blind people see, whether they are physically or spiritually blind. Please do a miracle in my life and help me to see clearly who you are. I also pray this for [say a friend's name]. Please help us not to have a hard heart which resists you. Amen.

Glory through suffering

Whoever wants to be my disciple must deny themselves and take up their cross and follow me.

Peter sees that Jesus is the Messiah – God's promised, rescuing King – but he only sees partially. With Peter's human perspective, he expected the Messiah to be a triumphant, warrior king, who would overthrow their enemies, the Romans. How does this compare with what Jesus says will happen? Jesus is a suffering King, who will be rejected and killed – the opposite of how we expect a king should be. No wonder Peter rebukes Jesus!

And what about those who would follow King Jesus? Jesus says they must follow in his footsteps. Not only will that mean denying themselves, but living Jesus' way may be like going willingly to execution. That's the force of the command to 'take up their cross' (8:34). How can such a decision be worth it? Because it will mean saving rather than losing your life: 'What good is it … to gain the whole world, yet forfeit their soul?' (8:36). When Jesus comes in his Father's glory, there will be no doubt that it has been worth it!

Peter, James and John then see a sneak preview of how Jesus is a glorious King. Up on a mountain, Jesus is transfigured before them, meaning that he is changed into a most glorious appearance – along with iconic leaders of the faith who have gone before. They hear how Jesus is the beloved Son of God, who will rise from the dead. News of Jesus' suffering and rising from the dead seems incredible, but the voice tells the disciples what to do: 'Listen to him!' (9:7).

We need to listen to Jesus too. The idea of denying ourselves is counter-cultural. But Jesus calls people to follow in his footsteps, to put saving our soul as we trust him above gaining what this world offers. Are there areas in your life where following Jesus' way will mean denying your own natural desires? Let's listen to Jesus' perspective, remembering he is the glorious Son of God, who promises that any suffering will be worth it in eternity.

KEY IDEA

Following Jesus involves listening to him and putting his way of living before our own.

PRAYER

Dear Jesus, thank you that you were willing to take up your cross, to suffer and to die for your people. Please help me to see how worthwhile it is to follow you, and to be willing to put you first in all areas of my life. Thank you for the glimpse of your glory in today's reading, seen even more clearly when you rose from the dead. Help me to grasp more of your power and glory, and to live my life with this in mind. Amen.

Who is your faith in?

I do believe; help me overcome my unbelief!

Peter, James, John and Jesus come down from the mountain to anarchy. A man whose son suffers from convulsions reports that the remaining disciples have failed to drive out an evil spirit and arguments abound. The disciples had previously driven out evil spirits (v. 13), so they are surprised that this one proves resistant (v. 28).

Jesus doesn't suggest that this demon is more resistant than others. Instead, he blames their unbelief (v. 19). Do the disciples not have enough belief? No, they seem to have much belief, but the problem is that it is in themselves! The boy's father, in contrast, directs his weak belief to Jesus as he says, 'I do believe; help me overcome my unbelief!' (v. 24). In response, Jesus drives out the evil spirit.

Why could the disciples not drive out the evil spirit themselves? Jesus explains, 'This kind can come out only by prayer' (v. 29). Prayer, asking God for help, involves depending on him. Prayer involves recognising our limitations and asking God to do what is humanly impossible. The disciples failed to do this.

I don't know if you feel you have strong or weak faith, but that is not as important as who our faith is in. We may feel we have weak faith, but let's lean on a strong, all-powerful God and demonstrate our dependence by asking him for help in prayer.

KEY IDEA

It is not the strength of our faith which matters, but the object of our faith.

PRAYER

Dear Jesus, thank you that you are more powerful than evil. I am conscious of my weakness, but please help me to depend on you day by day and to express this as I pray to you. I believe; help me to overcome my unbelief! Amen.

Radical action required

> *If your hand causes you to stumble, cut it off. It is better for you to enter life maimed than with two hands to go into hell, where the fire never goes out.*

Jesus is King of an upside-down kingdom! To be first in it, one must be a servant (9:35)!

His disciples argue about which of them is the greatest, yet Jesus has already told them twice that he, the King, would become the least and be killed (9:31). In God's Kingdom, the most insignificant, like a little child, is worthy of honour (9:37).

Thus it shouldn't be surprising that to cause a little one to sin (to go against God's ways, described as 'to stumble', 9:42) is a very serious thing in God's eyes. Indeed, anything causing us or others to sin is to be avoided at all costs. Jesus says we should be willing to cut off a hand or foot, or pluck out an eye, to avoid sinning. Does that seem harsh? Only if sinning is not a big deal. But God's kingdom is upside-down compared to the world's perspective. Jesus says that sin is serious and its consequences are eternal. The metaphors he uses to describe hell are shocking, but if the reality behind the metaphor is true, these verses are a loving warning. Because sin is so serious, we should take radical steps to avoid it.

Do you consider sin serious? Are you challenged by how serious Jesus takes marriage vows (10:1–12)? Many think that only a few extreme sins are serious, with most being perceived as naughty but nice. However, does it even depend on what we think? We need God, whom our sin offends, to tell us the truth. Jesus' message is that sin is deadly serious. But as we heed Jesus' warning, let's also heed his good news of rescue and forgiveness.

KEY IDEA

While our sin and rebellion against God is more serious than we often think, his offer of forgiveness is even more wonderful!

PRAYER

Dear God in heaven, please help me to grasp Jesus' loving warning about evil, sin and hell. Help me to avoid sin in all I say, think and do, and not to encourage others to sin either. Thank you that Jesus did not come to condemn, but to rescue us from this serious problem so that I need not fear death and hell. I pray in his name, amen.

Come like a child

> *... anyone who will not receive the kingdom of God like a little child will never enter it.*

What are children like when they are offered a free gift? Do they ask, 'Where's the catch?' or insist on paying? Or do they take it with both hands?! While it is often our role to teach children, Jesus says we can learn from them too: 'anyone who will not receive the kingdom of God like a little child will never enter it' (v. 15).

This is easier said than done, especially for the rich man who is confident he has kept God's commandments since he was a boy. Has he done enough to inherit eternal life in God's kingdom, to continue living after death in heaven?

Jesus says he must keep the commandments and lists some of the Ten Commandments given by Moses in the Old Testament. The man is feeling positive that he has kept these ... until Jesus tells him, 'sell everything you have and give to the poor' (v. 21). At this he goes away sad. Yes, he loves God and his neighbour a bit, but not that much. Jesus shows the man that he has not fully kept the commandments because he fails to love God above all else.

How much do you love God, compared to your love for money or other things?

Jesus observes, 'It is easier for a camel to go through the eye of a needle than for someone who is rich to enter the kingdom of God' (v. 25). Who then can be saved? No one – humanly speaking – unless we come to God like a child. We need to acknowledge we can never be good enough by ourselves because of the wrong things we do and say. Instead, we are invited to come to God with open hands, willing to receive eternal life as a free gift.

Have you come to God like a child, asking for the free gift of life forever which you do not deserve? Or are you trying to be good enough on your own merits, like the rich man?

KEY IDEA

Jesus offers us all the free gift of eternal life, but we need to be humble enough to accept it.

PRAYER

Dear heavenly Father, I know I am tempted to trust my own abilities rather than simply trusting you for acceptance. Please help me to come like a little child, humbly accepting your gift of a place in God's kingdom. Thank you that what is impossible for me to achieve by myself is made possible through your generosity and mercy. Please help me to follow your commands and teaching in grateful response. I ask this because of Jesus, amen.

The suffering, servant King

For even the Son of Man did not come to be served, but to serve, and to give his life as a ransom for many.

Jesus is on a mission which will culminate in Jerusalem. His determination to fulfil this mission is astonishing, particularly as he outlines for the third time (see also 8:31; 9:31) what will happen in Jerusalem – he will be condemned to death, mocked, spat upon, flogged and killed. But three days later he will rise again. Jesus is purposefully going to suffer.

Yet James and John haven't got suffering on their radar. Rather, they ask to sit beside Jesus in his glory (v. 37), meaning when he is one day seen by all to be reigning supreme. Have they grasped the suffering which Jesus will go through? All they see is glory, but Jesus knows that first he must drink a cup (v. 38). Here he is referring to Old Testament imagery of drinking a cup of God's wrath (see Jeremiah 25:15). Yes, Jesus will one day be seen in glory, but first whoever wants to become great must be a servant (v. 43).

How is Jesus going to serve? He has come to serve by giving up his life (v. 45). He will give up his life as a ransom so that many others can go free; many need to be ransomed or rescued from sin and its consequences (see 9:43–48).

How do you see your sin and its consequences? Do you understand that you deserve to drink the cup of God's wrath, but that Jesus intentionally suffered and gave his life so we don't have to do so? What an amazing King! Jesus is willing to serve and suffer to set undeserving people like us free!

How should we respond? Surely blind Bartimaeus is a good example to us. He cries out, 'Jesus, Son of [King] David, have mercy on me!' (v. 47).

KEY IDEA

We see Jesus as glorious when we see his suffering – how he gave up his life as a ransom for many. What a mercy!

PRAYER

Dear heavenly Father, thank you that Jesus was willing to be a servant and to suffer and give his life so that I need not face the punishment which my sins deserve. Help me to grasp more fully how sacrificial this was, and to respond as Bartimaeus did when Jesus called him. Amen.

How to produce spiritual fruit

Therefore I tell you, whatever you ask for in prayer, believe that you have received it, and it will be yours.

Jesus enters Jerusalem, the traditional home of the Israelite kings and the centre of Israelite worship, in a similar way to a king returning from battle. Except he isn't on a majestic horse ... but on a lowly colt. How is he received? Many people welcome him as King, perhaps seeing him as fulfilling an Old Testament prophecy (see Zechariah 9:9). But Jesus isn't focused on those who welcome him. Instead, he goes to the temple and shakes up many others in Jerusalem!

Why does the temple need a shake-up? What should be a 'house of prayer' has become a 'den of robbers' (v. 17) – people are profiting there rather than praying. Just as the fig tree is judged according to its lack of physical fruit, so God's people will be judged according to their lack of spiritual fruit; they are not producing evidence of a living faith.

What 'spiritual fruit' does God require from those who claim to follow him today? God's people should be depending on him in prayer rather than focusing on profit. They should have faith that he answers prayer (v. 23), and should be forgiving towards others while seeking forgiveness from God (v. 25).

How do you approach God in prayer? Is it a quick thought amid your busyness, or do you lay aside all distractions to depend on him? Do you pray primarily for monetary needs or for spiritual needs, such as the ability to trust God more and to be more forgiving?

Let's resolve to take time to pray intentionally to God, and for godly priorities as we pray. Graciously, he will answer that prayer (v. 24)!

KEY IDEA

If we claim to follow Jesus, that should show in our priorities, prayers and practice.

PRAYER

Dear heavenly Father, I know that, like many in Jesus' day, I am often self-centred and not genuinely prayerful or forgiving. Please help me, with your Holy Spirit, to be one of your people who takes time to pray and prioritises living in a way which pleases you. In Jesus' name, amen.

An authority stand-off

The stone the builders rejected has become the cornerstone ...

Jesus has been going around the temple acting like he owns the place (11:17). Who gave him that authority? He is asked this by those who believe they are the ones in authority. Jesus won't answer directly (11:33). Instead, he tells them a parable.

Jesus' parable answers the question of authority by referring to the Old Testament. Those listening will be familiar with how the prophet Isaiah used a vineyard as a metaphor for Israel (see Isaiah 5:1–7). The religious leaders know Jesus has 'spoken the parable against them' (12:12), who are like the tenants of the vineyard. What does Jesus accuse them of doing? They refuse to respect the owner of the vineyard – God. They dispose of the servants he sends to collect the fruit – who represent messengers from God, such as the prophets. Lastly, they plot to steal the vineyard by killing the son and heir. But what is the son's final destiny? He will be vindicated! The rejected stone will become a cornerstone, the most important stone holding together any structure (12:10).

So from where does Jesus claim his authority? He claims to be the son of the vineyard owner (God), who will be rejected but then glorified. You can't get a higher authority than that!

How might recognising Jesus' authority look for us? We should trust that his words are true, listen to him and obey his commands. For example, Jesus says to give to Caesar (the Roman ruler of the day) what he is due, and to God what is due to him (12:17). Submitting to human government and authority (when not in conflict with Jesus' authority) is a way of submitting to Jesus himself.

KEY IDEA

Jesus' authority is greater than all human authorities, in church or state. Praise him!

PRAYER

Dear God in heaven, thank you that you rule over everything. You made us and you love us. Thank you for sending your Son to die for us. Though he was rejected, he was in reality like a cornerstone – thank you for such a marvellous plan! Please help me to submit to his authority. As you also give us human authorities, I pray for our governments to rule wisely and fairly. Help us to honour them, but at the same time to submit all of our lives ultimately to you. In Jesus' name, amen.

Putting the Scriptures into practice

Love the Lord your God with all your heart and with all your soul and with all your mind and with all your strength.

How well do you know the Scriptures, the Bible? From today's passage, this isn't the most important question – it's applying it correctly to our lives that really matters.

How can we do this?

Firstly, read and apply the Scriptures correctly (vv. 18–27). The Sadducees, a Jewish sect, fail in this. They try to disprove the resurrection of the dead by suggesting a scenario which applies the Old Testament command that a man should marry his dead brother's wife (see Deuteronomy 25:5–6). At the resurrection, then, whose wife will she be, they ask. Jesus answers that there will be no marriage in eternity. But the bigger learning point is that the Sadducees fail to take account of the power of God or to read the Scriptures correctly. How can we understand the Bible correctly? By asking God for help, and by seeking wisdom from other thoughtful Christians such as friends, church leaders and writers.

Secondly, read and apply the Scriptures humbly (vv. 28–34). One teacher of the law asks which is the most important commandment. He agrees with Jesus that loving God and our neighbour is more important than outward ceremony, which serves to love our self. Jesus therefore comments that this man is 'not far from the kingdom of God' (v. 34). Let's expect the Bible to challenge our self-centred tendencies and to learn great things about God.

Thirdly, read and apply the Scriptures remembering Jesus (vv. 35–37). He is the key to how the 'son of David' (v. 35 – that is, a descendant of David) is in fact David's 'Lord' (v. 36) and the key to understanding all of the Bible!

Lastly, apply the Scriptures to daily life (vv. 38–44). How much do the teachers of the law allow the Scriptures to affect their lives? Not as much as an impoverished widow, who shows love for God in action.

Let's allow the Bible to affect how we spend our time, money and energy, as we love God above all else.

KEY IDEA

The most challenging part of reading God's word is not to understand it, but to put it into action.

PRAYER

Dear God in heaven, thank you for your written word in the Scriptures. Please help me to have a soft heart to listen and understand your word. Please show me if there are parts of Scripture which I am not putting into practice in my life. With your help, give me the desire and ability to follow your ways. For Jesus' sake, amen.

Be on your guard!

... the one who stands firm to the end will be saved.

What do you think when you hear of wars, earthquakes and famine? Does it make you think of the end of the world? Should it?

When Jesus tells his disciples that the magnificent temple will be destroyed (v. 2), this raises questions about the future. Jesus' answers are not straightforward to understand, but he gives several simple commands.

Should news of war take us by surprise? No. Jesus tells the disciples, 'do not be alarmed' (v. 7). Wars, earthquakes and famines are like 'the beginning of birth-pains' (v. 8) – pain which the world must go through before the end comes.

Nor is it just global trials they should anticipate. Jesus says the disciples should 'be on your guard' (v. 9). On account of following him, they will face persecution, arrest and trial before the good news of Jesus is preached to people from all nations. In the face of this hatred and betrayal, when they may be tempted to abandon their faith, how should they respond? By being 'one who stands firm' (v. 13).

History tells us about a terrible desolation when the magnificent temple was destroyed in AD 70, about forty years after Jesus' warning. In Jesus' words here, it's difficult to distinguish between when he is speaking of the temple desolation and of the end of time. However, the essential message is the same: 'be on your guard' (v. 23).

What does that command mean for us today? We should be prepared for the end of this world and alert to reminders that the end has yet to come. Wonderfully, if we are trusting Jesus (despite the opposition we face), we are as prepared as we need to be!

KEY IDEA

The one who stands firm to the end, looking to Jesus, will be saved.

PRAYER

Dear Lord Jesus, as your prediction of the destruction of Jerusalem came true, so we wait for you to fulfil your promises about the end. I pray that before that time, many people from all nations will hear of you. Please protect your followers who face wars, earthquakes, famine or spiritual dangers. May I be found safe that day, standing firm and trusting you in the face of any opposition or terror. For your glory I pray, amen.

Be alert!

Be on guard! Be alert! You do not know when that time will come.

What will the end of the world be like? When will it happen? We have so many questions. While Jesus doesn't always answer as we would like, he tells us how to be ready.

It's certainly going to be a dramatic event of cosmic significance. The world will be transformed (vv. 24–25). But what will the ultimate result be? The Son of Man (Jesus) will come in great power and glory, and gather his elect (those chosen by him) to safety (v. 27). From how Jesus earlier predicted the destruction of Jerusalem (vv. 14–19), as well as from other Bible passages, we know that Jesus returning will involve the final judgement and punishment for those who have failed to acknowledge him as Lord.

How, then, should we respond? Jesus has already instructed us to 'be on your guard' (vv. 9, 23), trusting him to rescue us from the coming judgement – a command he repeats in verse 33.

When will that great day be? Only the Father knows (v. 32). We do have some warning – just like a fig tree in leaf tells us summer is near, so desolations and persecutions tell us Jesus' coming is near (vv. 28–29).

How ought we to wait for a future but certain judgement? 'Be alert!' (v. 33). How do servants act as they wait for the sudden arrival of the master? They don't sleep; they get on with serving him while watching out for his return (v. 34). Everyone is instructed, 'Watch!' (v. 37).

How do we 'watch' today? There's no need to keep peering out the window – when Jesus returns, no one will miss him! But we ought to be ready by having Jesus as our master and by actively seeking to help others be ready too.

KEY IDEA

No one knows when Jesus will return, but this unknown is not a problem if we are ready.

PRAYER

Dear Lord Jesus, it can be daunting to wait for you to fulfil your promise to return to earth with great glory and power. Thank you that if we are alert and watchful, trusting in the salvation you offer, we do not need to fear your coming. Please may we be found safe, trusting you, on that great day. Please keep us alert and active in serving you as we wait. For your glory, amen.

Preparations

This is my blood of the covenant, which is poured out for many ...

The Passover was a Jewish festival, commemorating when God 'passed over' his people and rescued them from Egypt. It included a Passover meal where a lamb was eaten, remembering the lamb who died instead of the first-born in each Israelite house (see Exodus 12).

In today's passage, many are preparing for the Passover festival and meal, but some are preparing for events which would change the course of history...

Religious leaders prepare to kill Jesus (v. 1). When a woman expresses extravagant devotion to him, pouring expensive perfume on Jesus' head, they criticise her. Surely the money would have been better spent on people in need?! Yet Jesus declares her actions 'a beautiful thing' (v. 6). Why? The woman has prepared Jesus' body for burial (v. 8). We don't know if this was her intention, but clearly her sacrifice and devotion are appreciated by Jesus, who is preparing for his imminent death.

The disciples prepare for the Passover meal. But they aren't prepared for the news Jesus shares then – one of them will betray him. During the meal, Jesus is preparing for his suffering and glory. He distributes bread and wine as symbols of his body and blood which would soon be given up for many. But would his death be the end? Even before the betrayer acts, Jesus looks forward to another festival, another drinking of the fruit of the vine at a future heavenly banquet (v. 25).

Do you notice how Jesus uses each interaction as preparation for his suffering, death and future glory? What love he has for undeserving sinners that he becomes like a Passover lamb, giving up his life so others can go free! What love he has for us! Thank him!

KEY IDEA

Jesus' death is not an accident, but an intentional self-sacrifice – for the sake of others.

PRAYER

Dear Lord Jesus, thank you for being willing to suffer betrayal and death, to give your body and blood for many, to rescue us from the punishment which we deserve for our sin. Help me to understand the enormity of your sacrifice. Please help me to be devoted to you as sacrificially as the woman was, in response to your great love for me. Amen.

'Your will be done'

'Abba, Father,' he said, 'everything is possible for you. Take this cup from me. Yet not what I will, but what you will.'

You may know the phrase 'your will be done' from the Lord's Prayer, beginning 'Our Father', which Jesus taught his followers. This is fairly easy to pray when you want what God wants. But what if you know that God's will is that you should suffer and die in place of guilty people? Jesus knows this is God's plan for him, but prays, 'Yet not what I will, but what you will' (v. 36).

Jesus knows God's will from the Old Testament Scriptures. He is the shepherd who will be struck while sheep will scatter (v. 27).

His disciples are confident they will never abandon him (v. 31), but Peter, James and John can't even stay awake when Jesus asks them to watch and pray! Within a few hours they will all have fled (v. 50) and Jesus' prophecy will be fulfilled. Judas, one of the Twelve, betrays Jesus, handing him over to an armed crowd.

Jesus prays, 'Yet not what I will, but what you will' just before his arrest. Only Jesus fully grasps what is coming. Anticipating the cup of suffering he must drink causes him to be deeply distressed, troubled and overwhelmed with sorrow (vv. 33–34). Yet Jesus submits to the will of his Father.

What motivates you to complete tasks you would rather not do? Jesus is motivated by love. He loves and wants to obey his heavenly Father. He loves those for whom he will die.

Take time to reflect on how Jesus is willing to carry out the will of his Father, whatever the cost. What amazing love!

KEY IDEA

Jesus' will is to follow his Father's will, no matter what the cost.

PRAYER

Dear Lord Jesus, thank you that you were willing to face abandonment, betrayal and suffering, though you did not want to do so. I don't think I would have been any more faithful than the disciples. Please help me to understand more about what it cost you to carry out your Father's plan, and about your incredible love for people who had turned their backs on you. Amen.

On trial

... you will see the Son of Man sitting at the right hand of the Mighty One and coming on the clouds of heaven.

Innocent until proven guilty.

Whether this principle is accepted or not, now that Jesus has been arrested, the burden is on the prosecution to find him guilty. Why is this such a difficult task? They can't find any evidence against him (v. 55) and false testimonies do not agree (v. 56).

With just one question, though, the Jewish leaders get what they want. 'Are you the Messiah?' they ask (v. 61). For the first time, Jesus responds explicitly: 'I am. And you will see the Son of Man sitting at the right hand of the Mighty One and coming on the clouds of heaven' (v. 62).

Jesus declares himself as the Messiah – God's promised, rescuing King. Moreover, he declares himself the Son of Man who, according to the Old Testament prophet Daniel, would come on the clouds of heaven and be eternally worshipped by people from all nations (see Daniel 7:13–14).

Why is this a momentous statement? Jesus is declaring himself equal with God, a blasphemy worthy of death according to Jewish tradition.

Is he guilty of blasphemy? Not if what he says is really true!

Innocent until proven guilty? No. The innocent is simply declared guilty.

But if Jesus really is the one who will one day be seen in glory and worshipped by people from all nations, how should we respond? Are we tempted to be ashamed of him, as Peter is? Whenever we're tempted to disown or disobey Jesus, let's remember his identity. Jesus is God, the King of the universe – and one day everyone will see him for who he really is.

KEY IDEA

Jesus is 'guilty' of being the Messiah, who one day will return in glory with authority over those guilty of condemning him.

PRAYER

Dear Lord Jesus, how amazing it is that one day you will come on the clouds of heaven to be worshipped by all people! Yet you were willing to face false accusations and to be convicted as a guilty man. Thank you for such a costly sacrifice. Please help me to remember how you ultimately rule everything and so not to be ashamed to follow you. Amen.

The innocent for the guilty

> *Wanting to satisfy the crowd, Pilate released Barabbas to them. He had Jesus flogged, and handed him over to be crucified.*

Jesus may have been found guilty according to Jewish law, but how will a conviction of blasphemy be seen by the Romans, who are not concerned with offending the God of the Jews? The Jewish leaders will have to convince Pilate, the Roman governor, that Jesus' claim to be the Messiah is a threat to Roman authority. This is easier said than done, because Jesus is innocent!

Why does Jesus not defend himself against all the accusations? Is he refusing to give credence to any accusations? Is he helping to show Pilate and his accusers in their true colours? Or is he intending to be condemned? All of the above are true!

Jesus' enemies cannot find Jesus guilty of anything. In contrast, the prisoner Barabbas has been found guilty of insurrection and murder. However, due to pressure from the crowds, Jesus is condemned to death while Barabbas goes free.

It's an incredible substitution – an innocent King for a guilty gangster – which will transform the world!

This is incredible news for us because we are all guilty – perhaps not of insurrection, but guilty of being far from reaching the perfect standards of a holy God. Yet just as Barabbas is treated as innocent, so can we be! Jesus comes as an innocent substitute to die and so take the punishment which sinful people deserve. If we are willing, his death will count as the punishment for our sins so that we need not face that death sentence. This is mercy! This is a gift of boundless generosity! Have you gratefully received the gift?

KEY IDEA

Just as innocent Jesus takes the punishment of guilty Barabbas, he can also take the punishment which our sins deserve.

PRAYER

Heavenly Father, it is simply amazing to see how your Son was abused, mocked and unjustly condemned to death. I'm sorry because I have been guilty of mocking Jesus, both in my speech and in my attitude. Thank you that just as guilty Barabbas could go free, so Jesus' death means that I can be freed and escape punishment for my sin. Help me to understand this great exchange and rest in your forgiveness, which is possible because of Jesus. I ask in his name. Amen.

When Jesus dies ...

Surely this man was the Son of God!

'He saved others, but he can't save himself!' (v. 31). The mocking and insults continue, even from fellow criminals, after Jesus has been nailed to a cross. They see a thirsty, helpless man. Yet while Jesus is dying, Mark gives us other details to show us that something deeper and much more significant is happening.

Firstly, when Jesus dies, darkness comes over the whole land. Darkness in the Bible is symbolic of God's anger and judgement. Jesus feels forsaken by God (v. 34). Why? Just as Jesus has swapped places with the guilty Barabbas, so he is being treated by God as sinful, as deserving of anger and punishment.

Secondly, when Jesus dies, it is in his control. Jesus breathes his last while uttering a loud cry (v. 37). What does a deliberate final breath indicate? His life is not taken from him; he gives up his own life.

Thirdly, when Jesus dies, the curtain in the temple is torn in two, from top to bottom. The temple curtain acts as a barrier, separating people from God, just as sinfulness is a barrier between people and God. What is the significance of this curtain being removed? There is now no barrier between people and God! Anyone can approach God directly through Jesus, with the burden of their sin removed.

Lastly, when Jesus dies, a Roman centurion recognises him as the Son of God. Perhaps he had mocked Jesus just a few hours earlier, but seeing how Jesus dies is revolutionary.

What strikes you most about how Jesus dies? Pause to consider the significance of the details Mark gives us and thank Jesus for his self-sacrificial love.

KEY IDEA

Jesus can only save others if he does not save himself – what a Saviour!

PRAYER

Dear Lord Jesus, thank you that you did not come down from the cross and save yourself, but that you stayed up there to save others. Thank you that you faced the full judgement and punishment which my sin deserves, so that the barrier of sin between myself and God can be removed. Please help me to be like the Roman Centurion, understanding you are the Son of God. Help me to know the freedom and joy of a direct relationship with God as my Father. Amen.

He is risen!

He is going ahead of you into Galilee. There you will see him, just as he told you.

Their Messiah has died. Jesus' friends grieve. But this is not the end. Rather, it's the end of the beginning.

Jesus' death causes Joseph, a prominent Jewish leader but also an undercover follower of Jesus, to show his true allegiance. He is waiting for the kingdom of God (15:43), but why declare his faith in Jesus publicly now? We can't be sure, but perhaps something about how Jesus died has prompted Joseph to risk his reputation and be known as Jesus' follower. Following Jesus can be costly, but Joseph feels it is worth it.

Do you?

The grieving women rise early when the Sabbath is over to anoint Jesus' body. Yet they don't get a chance to do so. Instead of a dead man, they find a young man dressed in white. Their emotions go from grief, to alarm, to trembling fear as their expectations are confounded. Should they have responded differently? The young man gently reminds them that Jesus had told them this would happen – that he said he would rise again and go ahead of them into Galilee (14:28).

Everything has happened as Jesus said it would, including a mind-boggling resurrection from the dead! How much credence do you give Jesus' words? If his prediction of death and life again came true, surely we can trust every other statement!

The women must have later got over their shock and silence and told the disciples the young man's message, as instructed.[3] They in turn teach how Jesus' resurrection shows there is life beyond the grave for all who trust in Jesus.

Jesus has conquered death! Praise him, because he is alive today!

KEY IDEA

Jesus has died and risen again, just as he said he would. As these words came true, how much more can all his other words be trusted.

PRAYER

Dear heavenly Father, thank you that Jesus' words came true, that he rose from the dead. Help me to believe this incredible miracle and to understand what it teaches me about Jesus. Help me to be like the women and Joseph, willing to put Jesus before my own interests, as I wait for him to be seen by all as King of your kingdom. Thank you for all I have learned about Jesus in Mark's Gospel. Please help me to understand fully what it means to repent and believe in him. I pray in Jesus' name, amen.

3 Mark 16:9–20 is not in the earliest manuscripts we have of Mark's Gospel, and it is assumed that it was added later by others. As it is not widely recognised as part of Mark's Gospel, it is best to conclude with the ending of which we are more certain.

Glossary

Centurion – a Roman military officer in charge of one hundred soldiers.

Chief priests – Jewish religious leaders who operated the sacrificial system in the temple.

Christ – Greek form of Messiah, meaning 'anointed one'. The Old Testament Scriptures promised a Messiah who would be a rescuing king.

Council – a Jewish court, lower in status than the Sanhedrin.

Elijah – a great prophet in Israel.

John the Baptist – a relative of Jesus who prepared the way for him by baptising people in the wilderness as a sign of their repentance for their sin.

Herod – King Herod Antipas, ruler over the region of Galilee under the auspices of the Roman emperor. His father had been Herod the Great, who styled himself King of the Jews and split the kingdom between his three sons in his will.

Herodians – a Jewish group who supported the Herodian dynasty.

Kingdom of God – a spiritual kingdom whose subjects have God as their king. Jesus' first coming to earth ushered in the kingdom of God, which we see displayed partly now in the lives of God's people. God's kingdom will be fully established when Jesus comes again.

Leprosy – the word Mark uses which is translated as leprosy was used for a number of infectious skin diseases, not just the specific disease of leprosy. However, anyone with these diseases not only suffered that physical hardship but shared the same spiritual problem: they were declared spiritually unclean and therefore excluded from their community.

Messiah – Hebrew form of Christ, meaning 'anointed one'. The Old Testament Scriptures promised a Messiah who would be a rescuing King.

Moses – was commissioned by God to lead his people, the Israelites, out of slavery in Egypt. It was then to Moses that God gave the Jewish laws, including the Ten Commandments.

Mustard seed – what Mark 4 refers to is not the stuff children grow with cress on blotting paper and put in egg sandwiches! Jesus was instead referring to a shrub-like plant which produces seed pods containing very small seeds.

Nard – a plant that produced perfumes and ointments that were very costly and precious, as is the case in Mark 14.

Parable – a made-up story to teach a point. Jesus often taught using parables with hidden meanings.

Passover and Festival of Unleavened Bread – a major festival to commemorate God's rescue of his people from Egypt.

Pharisees – a religious group within Judaism. They were known for rigorously observing the laws set out in the first five books of the Old Testament. They had developed guidelines to help interpret and apply the law, but these had become like an extra layer of rules.

Pilate – the man appointed by the Roman emperor as prefect or procurator of Judea. He was a military leader and was in command of the local battalion of the Roman army. He had the ultimate power in the region and any death sentences handed down by the Sanhedrin had to be ratified by him.

Rabbi – a respectful form of address for a teacher. In the time of Mark's Gospel, it doesn't mean someone formally ordained as a Jewish religious leader, like it does today.

Repent – to be sorry for your sin, to turn away from your old, sinful way of living and to live in future for God.

Sabbath – the seventh day of the week, which is our Saturday today. In the Ten Commandments, God gives this law about the day: 'Remember the Sabbath day by keeping it holy. Six days you shall labour and do all your work, but the seventh day is a sabbath to the LORD your God. On it you shall not do any work, neither you, nor your son or daughter, nor your male or female servant, nor your animals, nor any foreigner residing in your towns. For in six days the Lord made the heavens and the earth, the sea, and all that is in them, but he rested on the seventh day. Therefore the Lord blessed the Sabbath day and made it holy' (Exodus 20:8–11).

Sadducees – a religious group within Judaism. They were similar to the Pharisees, but had a different understanding of some of the laws and didn't believe in the afterlife.

Sanhedrin – the highest Jewish court.

Synagogue – this word literally means 'gathering'. In Mark's Gospel, it is a meeting place for Jews to worship and where the Scriptures would be read and taught.

Teachers of the law – people who taught others about the Jewish law found in the first five books of the Bible. See also Pharisees and Sadducees.

Temple – the place where God was specially present with his people. The inner sanctuary of the temple was called the Holy of Holies and only priests could enter it. The temple was the focus of worship for the Jews and all would gather there to observe certain festivals such as the Passover and the Feast of Unleavened Bread. Animal sacrifices for purification and atonement for sin took place at the temple.